HotTips
for Speakers

25 Surefire Ways
to Engage and Captivate
Any Group or Audience

ROB ABERNATHY and MARK REARDON

Zephyr Press
Tucson, Arizona

About *Zephyr Press* . . .

Founded in 1979 in Tucson, Arizona, Zephyr Press continually strives to provide quality, innovative products for our customers, with the goal of improving learning opportunities for all. Our professional development line serves our commitment to lifelong learning. Other Zephyr Press material focuses on gifted education, multiple intelligences, and brain-compatible learning—tools to help *all* learners reach their highest potential.

HotTips for Speakers: 25 Surefire Ways to Engage and Captivate Any Group or Audience

Professional Growth

© 2002 by Rob Abernathy and Mark Reardon

Printed in the United States of America

ISBN: 1-56976-144-2

Editing: Kirsteen E. Anderson
Design & Production: Dan Miedaner
Illustrations: Ellen Duris
Cover: Dan Miedaner

Published by:
Zephyr Press
P.O. Box 66006
Tucson, Arizona 85728-6006
www.zephyrpress.com
www.i-home-school.com

Library of Congress Cataloging-in-Publication Data

Reardon, Mark, 1957-
    HotTips for speakers: 25 surefire ways to engage and captivate any group or audience / by Mark Reardon and Rob Abernathy.
        p. cm.
    Includes bibliographical references.
    ISBN 1-56976-144-2 (paperback)
    1. Public speaking I. Title: Hot tips, twenty-five surefire ways to engage and captivate any group or audience. II. Abernathy, Rob, 1953- III. Title.

PN4121 .R424 2001
808.5'1—dc21   2001024066

Dedication

This book is dedicated to our firstborn children, Brooke Danielle Abernathy and Noah Alexander Reardon. Thanks for the joy, inspiration, teachable moments, and memorable stories you bring to our lives daily. We love you!

To Cindy Abernathy, thank you for your careful editing of all my journeys and challenges. Your gentle love and friendship have become a map of support, with generous displays of inspiration, compassion, love, and care.

To Lynn Reardon, thank you for your honesty, your friendship, and your love. You continually demonstrate an unwavering commitment to our relationship and an undying faith in new possibilities.

Acknowledgments

To those who have taught us, led a seminar we have attended, or written a book we have read—we say a heartfelt "thank you." You have indeed inspired us!

We especially acknowledge the contributions of Rich Allen, Thomas Armstrong, Suzanne Bailey, Andrew Bisaha, Brian Blackstock, Robin and Kathy Bocchino, Glen Capelli, Michael Carr, Art Costa, Bobbi DePorter, John Dyer, Robert Garmston, Madeline Hunter, Eric Jensen, Spencer Kagan, George Keplinger, David Lindquist, Laurie Robertson, Blair Singer, Susan Smith, Michael Wall, Jeannie White-Murphy, and the following organizations: ASCD, IAL, NAESP, and NSDC.

About the Authors

Rob Abernathy is CEO of Intertainment, a consulting firm that sponsors seminars on curriculum development, accountability in education, and assessment issues. He holds a master's degree in educational administration and has extensive experience facilitating trainings for educators. He is coauthor of the *HotTips* series.

Mark Reardon is president of Centre•Pointe Education, culminating twenty-one years of experience as a teacher, principal, and educational consultant. Throughout, his focus has remained on discovering what works in teaching and learning. He has taught learners of all ages, from children to university professors, parents to CEOs. He is coauthor of *Quantum Teaching: Orchestrating Student Success* and the *HotTips* series.

Where to Find Stuff

Introduction

Many presenters, teachers, facilitators, and speakers feel the thrill of watching others learn. Since you picked up this book, you are probably one of them. And like so many teachers, public speakers, musicians, actors, and other performers, your satisfaction comes when your audience enjoys what you are doing as much as you do.

What Are HotTips?

HotTips are a collection of strategies that have worked for us, have worked for our friends, and will work for you. In this book you will find valuable techniques and strategies for public speaking, presenting, teaching, training, and facilitating. These tips get results.

Most tips are our original ideas, although some are adapted or borrowed from other sources. Each HotTip has been tested and used with audiences of all ages and all levels of experience. They add value to the orchestration and delivery of your information. We offer these HotTips as tools. We hope they will validate and enhance what you already do effectively. Try them all, then take the ones that work best for you and integrate them into your own tool kit of great ideas. Or try the following two exercises to identify what *you* most want to know. Once you identify your key questions and priorities, look for the tips that meet your most immediate needs and practice them first. As you continue to improve your skills, you may want to revisit your questions and priorities before selecting further tips to practice.

Top Five List

Imagine that sitting in front of you are the ten premier public speakers and trainers in the entire world. They have been invited to share everything and anything you have ever wanted to know about effective presentations. They have graciously granted you the opportunity to ask your top five most burning questions. What are the five most important questions that you would ask this group of professionals? Please write them below.

1. _____
2. _____
3. _____
4. _____
5. _____

Unpacking the Essence

What do you consider to be the seven most important characteristics of an effective presenter?

1. _____
2. _____
3. _____
4. _____
5. _____
6. _____
7. _____

What Is a HotTips Book?

A HotTips book is

➤ an effective tool that makes learning and information come alive through interactive text and activities

➤ an artfully designed workbook with space for you to record your thoughts, writings, drawings, and personal interactions

➤ an information-to-knowledge-to-application tool that provides relevant, brain-friendly, and immediately applicable strategies

➤ a collection of innovative and foundational information that will enhance your effectiveness as a communicator, whether you are facilitating a small group or lecturing in a giant hall

This HotTips book will enhance your skill integration and implementation. It will amplify your natural abilities by helping you tap into your knowledge, experience, and creativity while capitalizing on brain-compatible learning strategies. The activities take you beyond information to integration and application. As you work with the design, you will experience the way it becomes smart, relevant, and useful. The more actively you engage yourself with the activities and applications, the more valuable this book becomes.

Look for more books in the HotTips series. *HotTips for Teachers* is full of handy tips to help teachers hold students' attention and maximize learning. Also look for a book of HotTips specifically geared to group facilitation.

How Is This HotTips Book Organized?

The following pages preview the layout of this HotTips book and how you will use it. Each HotTip follows the same format, with icons to guide you to specific information. So grab a colored pen or pencil, or perhaps a highlighter. Leave your fingerprints on these pages through your pictures, symbols, words, color, and reflective thoughts. Then feel the impact of each HotTip on your next presentation.

Each section title is the name of a HotTip. Although we have attempted to group the tips logically, the order does not necessarily reflect the order in which you will utilize the tips during a presentation nor their relative importance.

The HotTip is defined in an action phrase that distills its essence in easily remembered language.

Between the quotation marks is an affirmation designed to strengthen your internal beliefs. Say this thought often.

Making It Mine is designed specifically to build skill integration. It contains brain-compatible learning strategies that help you implement the HotTip and cement it into your repertoire. This section will take you well on your way toward mastery!

Circle or mark the stars in Reach for the Stars as an iconic bar graph to chart your mastery of the HotTip! They represent stages of your development with this HotTip. The lower star represents initial implementation, the middle star a feeling of progress, and the top star competence. Three stars mean you are on top of this HotTip!

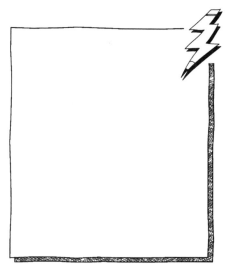

Draw an icon or write key words that represent the meaning of the HotTip for you.

Thinking It Over provides a place to reflect on what you have learned. If you are too busy to reflect, you are too busy to grow. Think about it!

You will find one of our favorite quotations or personal sayings in this box. Feel free to incorporate it into your repertoire.

Let Your Journey Begin!

As you start, bring along

- ➤ an appetite to bring joy and fun into learning
- ➤ an openness to have your passion stirred
- ➤ a willingness to find room in your existing tool kit for new thoughts and ideas
- ➤ blocks of time when you can interact and flow with the information
- ➤ your desire to ignite a new vision
- ➤ a successful, positive, natural you

Here are a few reflective questions to accelerate your growth:

- ➤ How effective am I as a presenter, teacher, trainer, or facilitator?

  _____

  _____

  _____

- ➤ What can I do today to dramatically transform the way I deliver information tomorrow?

  _____

  _____

  _____

This book is about your transformation into a memorable, persuasive, productive, effective, and relevant presenter of information. It is time to begin!

Project Confidence

Take a moment to access your inner confidence and enthusiasm, and project them through your posture and stance.

Your thoughts and feelings are manifested through your movement and posture. One of the first things your audience will notice is your posture. Why? Of all the information that floods the brain, 90 percent is visual, accounting for some 600 messages per second (Jensen 1995). Your movement and stance give your audience important clues as to how you are feeling and what you are thinking. If you are nervous and afraid, your audience will immediately recognize the signs in your stance. Conversely, you can consciously project an image of self-confidence and competence!

Before you begin your presentation, even before you approach the podium, access a resourceful state of confidence, enthusiasm, and authenticity. Take a deep breath. Reach inside and tap into the knowledge, skills, and beliefs on which your self-confidence is grounded. Smile and let your body express this inner state.

I will prepare from the inside out, accessing my passion and releasing joy, assurance, and confidence.

Making It Mine

One way to access a strong, resourceful state is to create it before you need it. First, list the feelings you experience during a successful presentation. Then write down things you see, and most important, what you say to yourself.

Feelings: _____

_____

I see: _____

_____

I tell myself: _____

_____

Now reread the list and place yourself in this successful scenario. Breathe deeply and clench your fist. Repeat this visualization three times, clenching your fist each time. The next time you need your resourceful state, think of this moment, breathe, and clench your fist.

Reach for the Stars!

Use the stars below to monitor your progress.

I have this tip down cold!

It is familiar territory.

This tip feels like a new pair of shoes.

In the box, draw an icon or write key words that represent Project Confidence.

Thinking It Over

Rewrite the metacognitive statement from page 7. Enlarge or bold key words or phrases.

_____

_____

_____

_____

_____

Record any enhancements you have made to Project Confidence, as well as your plans for implementing this HotTip.

Enhancements: _____

_____

_____

_____

_____

Implementation plans: _____

_____

_____

_____

_____

Private victories precede public victories.

—Stephen Covey

Enter Their Space

Use physical and mental strategies to accelerate relationships.

Approaching the front of the room and establishing rapport is an important journey. Every eye is on you. Every person is watching, forming opinions, creating assumptions, and seeking to validate initial perceptions. How do you maximize this moment? How can you establish a positive relationship with participants? By entering the audience's space, their mental and physical worlds.

To enter their mental world, stand in the participants' shoes, thinking and perceiving what they do. What needs, concerns, hopes, fears, experiences, and questions will they bring with them as they walk through the door? In their minds, what will make this event meaningful and relevant?

You can enter their physical world through varying degrees of proximity. Here's how: After you have been introduced, take the traditional spot in the front of the room. From there, thank and acknowledge the sponsor and the audience for their time, commitment, and presence. Then, pause, make eye contact, and take a step toward the group (entering their space). From this new spot you have a few options. (1) You might tell them the benefits and global outcomes of your presentation (enter their cognitive space). For example, "During our time together, you'll glean an updated perspective about how our brains function during the learning process. The fresh viewpoint will help the people you work with to comprehend, retain, and transfer their new learning."

(2) Through enrolling questions, you might tap into their anticipations or hesitations (enter their psychological space). For example, "How many of you are looking forward to a day of learning and fun?" or "Raise your hand if you are thinking, 'Here goes another training session.'" or "How many of you are here because it was someone else's good idea?"

By moving away from the traditional "speaker's spot," you'll shatter the stereotypical images of dry, staid, monotonous speeches delivered from behind a podium. In addition, this subtle yet powerful tip begins to forge a connection between you and your audience. Participants gain an appreciation of the real person, up close and personal, while you are building bridges into their world of expectations, anticipations, or hesitations.

 Entering the audience's space opens the way for increased rapport and connection.

Making It Mine

We believe that relationship is everything. It has become a critical link in the best practices of learning community models. To make this tip yours, ask, "What can I do in the opening moments that will continue building rapport beyond that  one small step?" Here's an extra HotTip: Continue getting into the audience's space! You will be amazed how this relational proximity strategy will mesmerize your participants as they tune into your every move. They will watch you simply because they want to know where you are going to move next, and what you are going to say when you get there.

Here are a few strategies we like to use:

➤ Tell a story, moving and speaking from various spots in the room.

➤ Do an enjoyable activity to enhance memory, moving and imagining objects and facts around the room. (See pages 57 and 105 for ideas.)

➤ Move from table to table, posing questions.

➤ Use the floor as a visual time line, plotting invisible dates along the length of the room or placing your outcomes along a continuum on the floor.

➤ Simply talk to your audience about the schedule for the presentation, moving farther into participants' space as you talk.

➤ Toss a Koosh elastic rubber ball or soft flying disk into the audience, offering the catching person an opportunity to ask a question. As you answer the question, move into the audience's space to retrieve the object.

Choose one of your own ideas, one of ours, or synthesize a few to create something new. Take a moment to design a strategy for implementing the Enter Their Space HotTip. A few moments of focus now will serve you a hundred-fold in your next speaking engagement. Go ahead now, and spin out some newness.

Reach for the Stars!

Use the stars below to monitor your progress.

I have this tip
down cold!

It is familiar
territory.

This tip feels like a
new pair of shoes.

In the box, draw an icon or write key words that represent Enter Their Space.

Thinking It Over

Rewrite the metacognitive statement from page 12. Enlarge or bold key words or phrases.

_____

_____

_____

_____

_____

HotTips for Speakers ©2002 Zephyr Press, Tucson, AZ • 800-232-2187 • www.zephyrpress.com

Record any enhancements you have made to Enter Their Space, as well as your plans for implementing this HotTip.

Enhancements:_____

_____

_____

_____

_____

Implementation plans:_____

_____

_____

_____

_____

> **When you walk to the podium, remember to take yourself along. That's the natural, energetic, forceful you that got you there.**
>
> —Tom Leech

Hold Eye Conversations

Hold eye contact with individuals in the audience for three to five seconds each.

Presentations, talks, speeches, and workshops are all forms of human interaction, and building rapport is vital. People like to feel that you are talking to them alone. Making purposeful eye contact says to your audience that you are interested not just in your content, but in them as people.

Presenters often look over the heads of the audience, or dart their eyes around the group. This sends a message of uncertainty or self-centeredness. Your audience wants to feel included, as if they were in a dialogue with you. Making eye contact makes them feel included in your ideas. It makes all the difference in their receptivity!

While addressing your audience, hold eye contact with one person at a time for about three to five seconds. Look into the person's eyes, as if you are talking directly to him or her. Then find another face and another set of eyes until you have held brief eye conversations with every participant in the room.

 I strengthen the relationship between the audience and myself by using eye contact as a gateway for rapport.

Making It Mine

Practice making eye contact with yourself in a mirror, timing yourself to get a feel for how long three to five seconds is. You will become increasingly comfortable with making eye contact the more you practice, so practice it daily.

Increase your awareness of when and for how long you hold eye contact with people. Start with your friends, and see what you notice. Make changes as appropriate. Then expand your practice to people at work, on the street, in the market, or in other public places. Sometimes it feels awkward to look into the eyes of another person while communicating, because in typical conversation, the person who is listening makes eye contact but the person who is speaking does not. Making eye contact is normally a signal that the speaker is ready to give the listener a turn to speak. During the next conversation you have with a friend, if making eye contact feels awkward, focus on just one eye at a time.

Reach for the Stars!

Use the stars below to monitor your progress.

I have this tip down cold!

It is familiar territory.

This tip feels like a new pair of shoes.

In the box, draw an icon or write key words that represent Hold Eye Conversations.

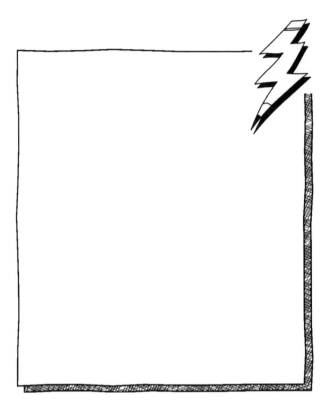

Thinking It Over

What works for you in holding eye contact?

_____

_____

_____

_____

_____

Record any enhancements you have made to Hold Eye Conversations, as well as your plans for implementing this HotTip.

Enhancements: _____

_____

_____

_____

_____

Implementation plans: _____

_____

_____

_____

_____

> **Presentations are a human relationship.**
>
> —Rob Abernathy

Invite Questions
with an Upward Palm

Use an upward palm, rather than a
pointed finger, when gesturing toward or
calling on a participant.

A palm-up gesture suggests openness and invitation. Softer, universal, and more appealing, it is an excellent replacement for the harshness of finger pointing. When you motion toward someone, hold your hand out and open, palm up at about a 45 degree angle—somewhat the way the pope does as he acknowledges a crowd of people. Motion smoothly toward the person as you nod and smile.

The gesture may feel a bit awkward at first, yet with a simple turn of your wrist you will send a warm message of invitation. This invitation beckons participant response. It communicates your desire to listen and your willingness to entertain ideas and alternative views.

 I use a gentle palm-up gesture to
invite participants' responses and
suggest openness to ideas.

Making It Mine

Practice the palm-up gesture now. Stand up and imagine yourself eliciting responses from an audience. Feel how natural it is to gesture in this way.

To experience the power of your palm, try the following two exercises.

First, go to a favorite clothing store for a little browsing. When the salesperson asks whether you need assistance, turn your palm out in a "stop" gesture and say, "No, thanks." Notice how much more effective the gesture and words are compared to the words alone.

Second, sit with a group of friends. Consciously and purposefully incorporate the palm-up gesture as you ask and respond to questions. Like a masterful conductor you can orchestrate the timing of the communication through the use of your palm.

Reach for the Stars!

Use the stars below to monitor your progress.

I have this tip down cold!

It is familiar territory.

This tip feels like a new pair of shoes.

In the box, draw an icon or write key words that represent Invite Questions with an Upward Palm.

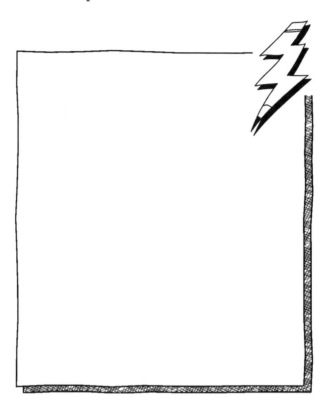

Thinking It Over

On the lines below, jot down the times in your next presentation when the palm-up gesture would be appropriate.

_____

_____

_____

_____

_____

Record any enhancements you have made to Invite Questions with an Upward Palm, as well as your plans for implementing this HotTip.

Enhancements:_____

_____

_____

_____

_____

Implementation plans:_____

_____

_____

_____

_____

> The courage
> to speak must
> be matched
> by the wisdom
> to listen.
>
> —Anonymous

Use Modality-Specific Language

Choose words and phrases that speak directly to the visual, auditory, and kinesthetic pathways.

Language has the power to access mental associations. You can facilitate deeper meaning and clearer understanding of your content by choosing words that resonate with different learning modalities (Ostrander and Schroeder 2000). Gain clarity as you *see* the following example, *hear* yourself saying the words, and *feel* their impact.

Visual: Use words that evoke seeing, pictures, or images. (See how this might sharpen the image of your presentation.)

Auditory: Use words that resonate with sounds or tones. (This technique rings true for your learners.)

Kinesthetic: Use words that capture touch, texture, or physical movement. (Explore how your words and phrases grab the attention of your learners.)

Tap into the visual, auditory, and kinesthetic modalities by choosing language patterns that speak in each modality.

I connect directly with learning modalities by consciously crafting my words and phrases to engage the visual, auditory, and kinesthetic modes of my participants.

Making It Mine

Think about the outcomes of an upcoming presentation. Create three sentences, one sentence per outcome. Use words and phrases that tap a different modality in each of the sentences. (Example: *Grasp strategies that increase retention.*)

Here is a word list to get you started.

Visual	Auditory	Kinesthetic
clear	*rings true*	*hold on to*
picture	*sounds like*	*touch the . . .*
view	*dialogue*	*feel the . . .*
glance	*listen*	*tools to use*

_____

_____

_____

_____

_____

_____

_____

Reach for the Stars!

Use the stars below to monitor your progress.

I have this tip
down cold!

It is familiar
territory.

This tip feels like a
new pair of shoes.

In the box, draw an icon or write key words that represent Use
Modality-Specific Language.

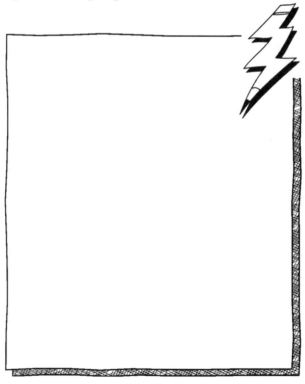

HotTips for Speakers ©2002 Zephyr Press, Tucson, AZ • 800-232-2187 • www.zephyrpress.com

Thinking It Over

Rewrite the metacognitive statement from page 25. Enlarge or bold key words or phrases.

_____

_____

_____

_____

Record any enhancements you have made to Use Modality-Specific Language, as well as your plans for implementing this HotTip.

Enhancements:_____

_____

_____

Implementation plans:_____

_____

_____

> ## Genius is the ability to reduce the complicated to the simple.
>
> —C. W. Ceran

Whisper

 Use a soft yet strong voice to make important points.

In each presentation, there are key phrases or statements, significant thoughts you want your audience to remember. Lowering your voice redirects focus. Therefore, you can enhance your participants' learning by purposely employing an undertone to make important points.

In the middle of a sentence, lean forward with an eager expression. Then drop your voice almost to a whisper and watch your audience lean in to hear your soft, deliberate intonation. The whisper capitalizes on the principle of using vocal variation for increased attention. Use this tip sparingly to maximize its effectiveness.

 In any presentation, I create two or three powerful moments that have immediate impact.

Making It Mine

Are you aware of the volume of your normal speaking voice? Most presenters are not. Increase your awareness by audiotaping your next speech or even your next conversation with a friend. Play the tape back, listening carefully to variations in tone, volume, and pacing. Write your findings and insights below:

_____

_____

_____

_____

_____

_____

_____

_____

_____

Reach for the Stars!

Use the stars below to monitor your progress.

I have this tip down cold!

It is familiar territory.

This tip feels like a new pair of shoes.

In the box, draw an icon or write key words that represent Whisper.

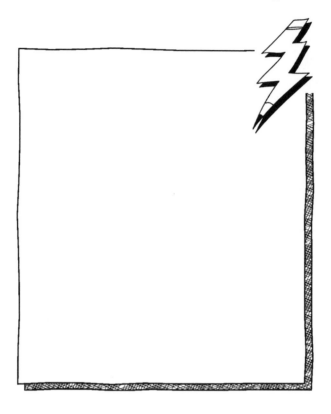

Thinking It Over

The next time you listen to a speaker, think of the moments in the delivery where he or she could have inserted a whisper. What impact would it have had?

_____

_____

_____

_____

_____

Record any enhancements you have made to Whisper, as well as your plans for implementing this HotTip.

Enhancements:_____

_____

_____

_____

_____

Implementation plans:_____

_____

_____

_____

_____

> If silence
> is golden,
> whispering
> is the
> silver lining.
>
> —Mark Reardon

Pause

 Interject a momentary silence to gain attention.

Faster than the spoken word, more powerful than an overhead, a pause quickly captures attention. Just before you make an important point, stop speaking for three to five seconds. Stand still, maintain eye contact, and appear contemplative, as if you are considering your next thought. The audience members will lean forward and tilt their heads in anticipation. Deliver that point with certainty, conviction, and passion.

Speakers often are so excited about the content they are presenting that they move quickly from point to point. Soon all points appear to be of equal value! You can punctuate key points by pausing. Purposefully pausing provides time for you to access your passion, gain attention, and deliver your message with congruence.

 I pause to reconnect my passion with my information.

Making It Mine

Think about an informational or inspirational section in an upcoming presentation. Now focus on the key statement or phrase. Write it below, placing spaces before key words.

_____

_____

_____

_____

_____

_____

_____

Now say the sentence or phrase aloud, pausing where you have indicated. Say it again, this time with vocal inflection for emphasis.

Reach for the Stars!

Use the stars below to monitor your progress.

I have this tip
down cold!

It is familiar
territory.

This tip feels like a
new pair of shoes.

In the box, draw an icon or write key words that represent Pause.

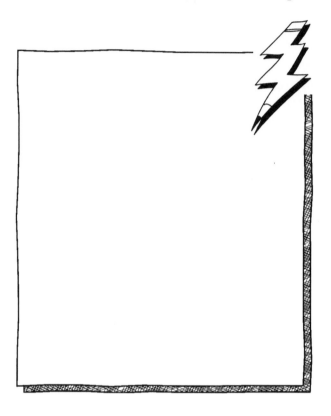

Thinking It Over

Rewrite the metacognitive statement from page 32. Enlarge or bold key words or phrases.

_____

_____

_____

_____

_____

Record any enhancements you have made to Pause, as well as your plans for implementing this HotTip.

Enhancements:_____

_____

_____

_____

_____

Implementation plans:_____

_____

_____

_____

" It is not so much knowing when to speak, as when to pause.

—Jack Benny **"**

Crest the Wave

Identify the moment when conversations peak.

Timing is everything! Just as a wave crests before it breaks onto the shore, so does the energy within a small-group discussion. As your participants share in such a group, the intensity of interaction peaks just before the group gets off track. Listen carefully to the overall speaking volume of a group. Notice that from the moment you give directions, the volume slowly increases until it reaches a crest. When the volume reaches this crest, ask participants to wrap up their discussion. By doing so, you guide the energy of the group before it dissipates to off-topic conversations.

Crest the Wave is a premier facilitation skill originally described by Rich Allen in his *Training Manual for SuperCamp Facilitators*; he has graciously allowed us to share it with you. Knowing when to move from small- to large-group discussions distinguishes the good facilitators from the best. Be aware of the rise and fall of the group's dynamics, and move to the next activity when the volume reaches a crest.

During small-group interactions, I listen carefully for the crest of the discussion, then redirect participants' focus.

Making It Mine

The next time you are around a group of people, sit with purposeful attention and listen. Listen to the fluctuation in voices and noises. Listen to the ebb and flow of the conversations. Listen to the volume, pacing, and moments of silence in the group interaction. Challenge yourself to anticipate the crest in the dialogue. Listen to the rhythms of the underlying message. Make listening beyond the words an enjoyable challenge.

Where are good places to eavesdrop? Try this at a park, mall, coffee shop, restaurant, or party.

_____

_____

_____

_____

_____

Reach for the Stars!

Use the stars below to monitor your progress.

I have this tip down cold!

It is familiar territory.

This tip feels like a new pair of shoes.

In the box, draw an icon or write key words that represent Crest the Wave.

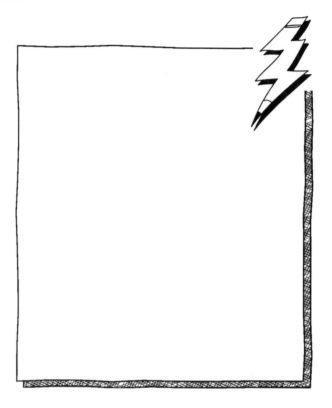

Thinking It Over

Why do you think conversations crest?

_____

_____

_____

_____

_____

Record any enhancements you have made to Crest the Wave, as well as your plans for implementing this HotTip.

Enhancements:_____

_____

_____

_____

_____

Implementation plans:_____

_____

_____

_____

_____

> We don't need
> more strength
> or more ability.
> What we need
> is to use
> what we have.
>
> —Basil S. Walsh

Do the Ninja

Avoid creating a distraction by walking slowly within the learning environment.

Frequently, you may need to move to another part of the room while participants are engaged in an individual or group task. You may even need to do so while your partner is presenting. Walk slowly, like a Ninja, so as not to cause a disturbance. Maintain your focus either on your partner, if he or she is presenting, or on the written directions at the front of the room. Anyone whose attention drifts to you will notice your calm movements and your focus at the front. That person's focus will shift to where you are looking. This HotTip works well with small and large audiences.

When you are a speaker or facilitator, people will naturally look toward you, no matter where you are in the room. Since "where the attention goes, the energy flows," direct your attention to where you want participants' attention to be. How do you know you have done the Ninja? When no one really notices!

 I move with focus and grace, respecting the atmosphere of learning.

Making It Mine

A great side effect of the Ninja technique is that it helps you relax, catch your breath, and gain a different perspective on the room. Before your next presentation, consciously monitor the speed at which you walk, brush your teeth, or move to answer the telephone. Practice moving a bit more slowly and taking deeper breaths as you do.

Take a moment to consider moments in your next presentation when Do the Ninja would be useful. Write one of those moments below.

_____

_____

_____

_____

_____

Reach for the Stars!

Use the stars below to monitor your progress.

I have this tip down cold!

It is familiar territory.

This tip feels like a new pair of shoes.

In the box, draw an icon or write key words that represent Do the Ninja.

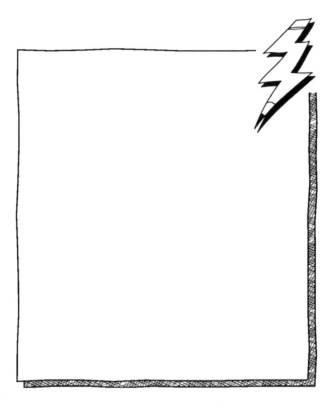

Thinking It Over

Rewrite the metacognitive statement from page 40. Enlarge or bold key words or phrases.

_____

_____

_____

_____

_____

Record any enhancements you have made to Do the Ninja, as well as your plans for implementing this HotTip.

Enhancements: _____

_____

_____

_____

_____

Implementation plans: _____

_____

_____

_____

_____

> **People forget how fast you did a job— but they remember how well you did it.**
>
> —Howard W. Newton

Hang the Flip Charts

 Post flip charts on the walls to maximize incidental learning.

During many presentations, you may use flip charts to record key points, useful lists, diagrams, and graphic organizers. At the break, place these flip-chart posters on the walls. Post them above your head, either on the front wall or on the side walls near the front of the room. As people look around the room throughout the training, their retention will be increased through peripheral learning.

Studies show that the use of peripherals increases long-term retention by as much as 80 percent (Jensen 1995, 55–58). This is especially true when the posters contain symbols or pictures relating to or representing the content. Here is a poster-making tip: Write important words or phrases in large, bold letters. Example: ▶

EVERYTHING
is done on
PURPOSE!

" I post key ideas on the walls to strengthen retention. "

Making It Mine

Consider the two or three key concepts of your next presentation. Write them on the flip charts below. Remember to make the important words stand out by making them larger or bolder, or by writing them in different lettering or a different color.

Reach for the Stars!

Use the stars below to monitor your progress.

I have this tip
down cold!

It is familiar
territory.

This tip feels like a
new pair of shoes.

In the box, draw an icon or write key words that represent Hang the Flip Charts.

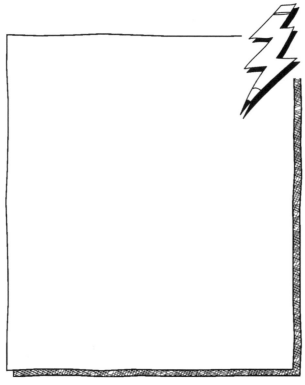

Thinking It Over

Record one goal you would like to pursue. Write it on four or five sticky notes. Post the notes in places where you will look at them often, such as in your car, in your office, or on your bedroom mirror. Let these mini-flips become your daily reminders of the goal you are achieving.

_____

_____

Record any enhancements you have made to Hang the Flip Charts, as well as your plans for implementing this HotTip.

Enhancements: _____

_____

_____

Implementation plans: _____

_____

_____

> Unless you try
> to do something
> beyond what you
> have already
> mastered, you
> will never grow.
>
> —Ralph Waldo Emerson

Post Truth Signs

Post statements about learning and life
to reinforce participants' internal beliefs.

People's success in learning rests on the beliefs they hold about themselves as learners. Amplify your participants' beliefs by posting positive truths about the learning process. As you create these signs, remember to write key words in large, bold letters. Place these truth signs on the side walls at the eye level of seated participants. As audience members read the statements, their internal belief structures will be enhanced.

Here are a few truths to get you started:

➤ We all are gifted; some of us just open our packages earlier than others.

➤ For things to change, I must change.

➤ Everyone needs time to think and learn.

➤ We can do more and learn more when we are willing to risk.

Reminders are powerful. Even though the response might be, "Oh, I know that," the truth statement puts reality back into focus.

By strengthening beliefs, I empower my audience to become lifelong learners.

Making It Mine

You probably have truth sayings you use in your personal or professional life. Capture a few of your favorites below. Decide which one or ones you will post first, and how you will introduce each to your audience.

_____

_____

_____

_____

_____

These truth signs are effective in a presentation or facilitation context:

- ➤ I am a capable and confident presenter.
- ➤ Powerful learning welcome here!
- ➤ Learning is an experiential journey.
- ➤ Process is important. Reflection is even better.

Reach for the Stars!

Use the stars below to monitor your progress.

I have this tip down cold!

It is familiar territory.

This tip feels like a new pair of shoes.

In the box, draw an icon or write key words that represent Post Truth Signs.

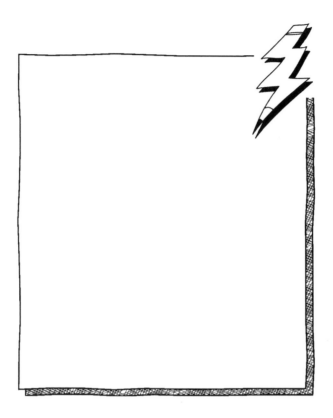

Thinking It Over

To put yourself on the edge of a new mental model, ask yourself this question: "What is impossible for me to do as a presenter that, if I could do it, would fundamentally change the way I present?"

_____

_____

_____

_____

_____

Record any enhancements you have made to Post Truth Signs, as well as your plans for implementing this HotTip.

Enhancements:_____

_____

_____

_____

_____

Implementation plans:_____

_____

_____

_____

_____

> ❝ Learning is
> like gelatin.
> It sets
> the way you
> mold it.
>
> —Mark Reardon ❞

Share Autobiographic Metaphors

Tell a short autobiographic story containing associations to what participants will be learning.

Near the beginning of your presentation, share a personal or professional incident pertaining to the topic you are addressing. Weave into this story metaphors for the learning process or the upcoming content. For example, here is a story that prepares the audience to approach a new learning experience with a sense of adventure and discovery:

One of my favorite pastimes is mountain biking, especially on new trails. Even though I know my bike and my own ability, there is always some challenge of the unknown. Will there be any ruts on the trail? Any fallen trees? Any boulders resting in the path? How many sharp turns are there? Most important, where are the beautiful spots? What will I see and experience that I have not done before? Despite these uncertainties I know that the accomplishment will be worth the effort, discomfort, and slight nervousness. Today's seminar may be a new trail for some of you. It may lead you into new territory. And even though the experience may be challenging, you will find your ability and experience enhanced.

The brain communicates in metaphoric, symbolic language. In other words, it stores information as associative images and it constructs meaning based on the images it makes. By creating associations, you lay the groundwork for the learning to come. Moreover, by telling your story you build rapport. Have you ever noticed how people perk up when a story is told? There is something innately intriguing about a story. Use this to your advantage. Capitalize on learners' interest and embed in your story metaphors you can draw on later.

 I build rapport and credibility when I share an autobiographical story infused with metaphors.

Making It Mine

Have you ever had a day so full of challenges that you said to yourself, "I can't believe this is happening to me?" There is probably a good story there! Think of incidents that happened while on vacation, with the family, out with friends, growing up, caught in an embarrassing moment, or driving in the car. Write down any ideas you have.

_____

_____

_____

_____

_____

_____

_____

_____

Reach for the Stars!

Use the stars below to monitor your progress.

I have this tip
down cold!

It is familiar
territory.

This tip feels like a
new pair of shoes.

In the box, draw an icon or write key words that represent Share Autobiographic Metaphors.

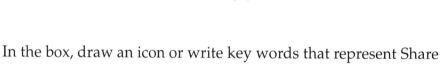

HotTips for Speakers ©2002 Zephyr Press, Tucson, AZ • 800-232-2187 • www.zephyrpress.com

Thinking It Over

One challenge you face as a presenter is reaching multicultural audiences. Four healing and restorative elements are common to all cultures: storytelling, singing, dancing, and silence. How can you incorporate these elements into your next presentation?

Storytelling: _____

_____

Singing: _____

_____

Dancing: _____

_____

Silence: _____

_____

Record any enhancements you have made to Share Autobiographic Metaphors, as well as your plans for implementing this HotTip.

Enhancements: _____

_____

Implementation plans: _____

_____

> Every job is
> a self-portrait
> of the person
> who did it.
>
> —Anonymous

Walk to Remember

Move to a different spot to jog your memory.

Have you ever forgotten what you were going to say? So have we! Even the most seasoned presenters suffer from temporary mind-freeze. When you have a mental lapse, take a deep breath and move from the spot where you are stuck. As you move your body, your mind shifts as well, jogging your memory. From the audience's perspective you are simply changing positions. From your perspective, you are unlocking your next thought.

The mind and body are connected. When you move your body, you move your mind. (The reverse is also true!) This is an especially useful tip if you memorize key parts of your presentation. Lock these important thoughts in your body with a physical motion— a hand gesture, arm motion, tilt of the head. As you move from point to point in your presentation, your body helps you to remember.

If I get stuck during a presentation, I remain calm, allowing my body to remind me of the next thought.

Making It Mine

A related mnemonic strategy is a mental floor plan. Let's use your living room as a tool. Imagine three key pieces of furniture in that room, such as a television, a couch, and a fireplace. Now think of the three key facts in your next presentation. Let's say these main ideas are flexibility, relationship, and leadership. Attach these facts to the three pieces of furniture. See the television twisted and stretched. (Flexible.) Imagine two lovers sitting on the couch building their relationship. (Relationship.) Visualize images of famous leaders warming themselves at the flames of the fire. (Leadership.)

Now simply take an imaginary walk through your living room. As you pass the twisted television, it immediately reminds you of flexibility. Pass the couch. What do you see? What does it remind you of? What about the fireplace? Can you see leadership in the flames? Exercise your mind by tapping into the skills of kinesthetic imagination.

Reach for the Stars!

Use the stars below to monitor your progress.

I have this tip down cold!

It is familiar territory.

This tip feels like a new pair of shoes.

In the box, draw an icon or write key words that represent Walk to Remember.

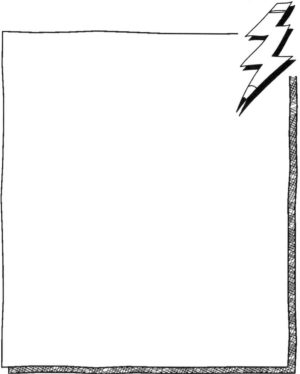

Thinking It Over

Which strategy works best for you? Using physical motions or a mental floor plan? Consider the first two points of your next presentation and attach each one to a body motion. As you practice your presentation, actually make each motion while saying the associated point. Next, do the motion and silently think the point. Record your associations to strengthen your memory.

Point 1: _____

_____

Movement: _____

_____

Point 2: _____

_____

Movement: _____

_____

Record any enhancements you have made to Walk to Remember, as well as your plans for implementing this HotTip.

Enhancements: _____

_____

_____

Implementation plans: _____

_____

_____

> Forget?
> I never forget
> my talk!
> What was
> your question?
>
> —Tom Ogden

Ignore the First Hand

Encourage thinking and avoid resistance by not calling on the first person to raise a hand.

Imagine that during your presentation you present a thought-provoking idea or challenge an existing paradigm. A hand shoots up just as you finish that thought-provoking, challenging comment. Your tendency may be to call on the first hand you see.

Instead, wait for a second and a third hand to go up. Call on anyone but the first person to raise a hand. That person is usually argumentative. (This is not necessarily true in the classroom or with a group that knows you.) Let others speak first, then call on the first person if his or her hand is still raised. If the person makes an emotionally charged comment or gives an opinion masked as a question, remember to breathe. Then thank the person for sharing those thoughts.

By waiting you increase everyone's thinking time and diffuse potentially hostile responses. Waiting allows the emotion to dissipate, giving people time to evaluate their initial thoughts. Waiting promotes quality and clarity of thought.

 I desire participation and welcome alternative viewpoints. I choose to provide thinking time by waiting.

Making It Mine

Most of us feel a little uncomfortable when
someone poses a challenging question or
offers a contrary opinion. How do you react?

Recall one of those moments and notice what happens to you
emotionally, physiologically, and mentally. Jot down your reactions.

Emotional: _____

Physiological: _____

Mental: _____

What will you do in the future when a similar situation arises?
What would be the advantage of a different response? Also
consider the motivation of the person asking the question. How
might this understanding help you craft your response?

I will do: _____

Advantage: _____

Motivation: _____

Reach for the Stars!

Use the stars below to monitor your progress.

I have this tip
down cold!

It is familiar
territory.

This tip feels like a
new pair of shoes.

In the box, draw an icon or write key words that represent Ignore the First Hand.

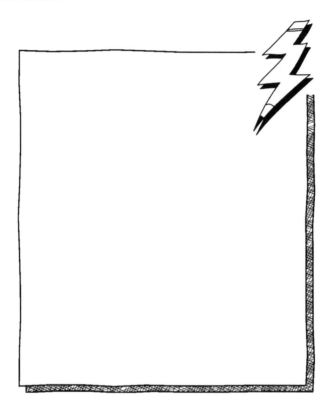

Thinking It Over

Imagine you are presenting to about 150 people. In the middle of your talk, an angry participant stands up and shouts, "This is stupid and boring; it doesn't work and you're wasting my time!" What would you do? Jot down your first response.

_____

_____

_____

_____

_____

Now, reflect on the situation. Consider your values and beliefs. What would you change about your initial response?

_____

_____

_____

What would be the most effective strategy for responding?

_____

_____

_____

Record any enhancements you have made to Ignore the First Hand, as well as your plans for implementing this HotTip.

Enhancements:_____

_____

Implementation plans:_____

_____

> **Seek first
> to understand,
> then to be
> understood.**
>
> —Stephen Covey

Memorize Names

Learn participants' names to build rapport.

Yes, people attend your speech, workshop, seminar, or class to hear your information. But they also come to interact with another person, namely you. Making personal contact with a large audience is a bit challenging. Here is a little tip with big returns.

Greet people as they arrive or when they first take a seat. Memorize the names of three or four people, preferably people with different characteristics (e.g., job position or title, experience, gender). During your presentation, use those names, perhaps in examples or when referring to conversations you had with those people. Not only will those individuals feel honored that you remembered their names, others will think you remembered theirs as well!

Here is a tip for memorizing names: As you shake hands, listen to the way the person says his or her name. Repeat the name in your head as you impose the first letter on the person's face.

I honor audience members by taking the time to learn their names.

Making It Mine

Begin practicing name memorization now. As a server in a restaurant or a salesclerk in a store waits on you, make a conscious effort to lock his or her name into your memory. Tie a distinguishing feature or mannerism to the name. Repeat people's names back to them as you greet them.

Take a moment and imagine a few of your friends. See their faces in your mind. Now take each person's first initial and place it on his or her face. Hear yourself saying the name aloud.

Reach for the Stars!

Use the stars below to monitor your progress.

I have this tip down cold!

It is familiar territory.

This tip feels like a new pair of shoes.

In the box, draw an icon or write key words that represent Memorize Names.

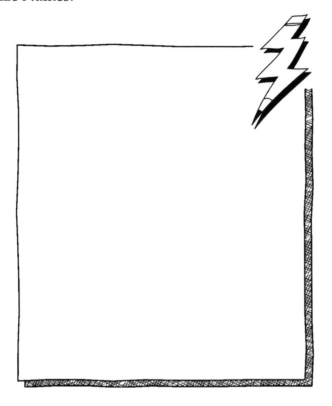

Thinking It Over

Rewrite the metacognitive statement from page 64. Enlarge or bold key words or phrases.

_____

_____

_____

_____

_____

Record any enhancements you have made to Memorize Names, as well as your plans for implementing this HotTip.

Enhancements: _____

_____

_____

_____

_____

Implementation plans: _____

_____

_____

_____

_____

> Security in life comes from knowing that every single day you are improving yourself in some way.
>
> —Anthony Robbins

Acknowledge Participants

Recognize audience participation and contributions.

Acknowledgments energize participants, set a positive tone, and promote lifelong learning (Goleman 1997). Add novelty and variety by introducing a variety of forms of acknowledgment. In addition to hearty clapping, use standing ovations, hoorays, finger snaps, drum rolls, and mini thank-you notes to recognize individual or group accomplishments.

Knowing when to acknowledge is very important in using this tip effectively. When given after some form of participation, acknowledgment strengthens risk-taking—a lifelong learning trait. Acknowledge people when they volunteer to come forward (especially if they do not know what they will be asked to do!) and when they provide a particularly astute insight. Give acknowledgment before and after individual and small-group presentations. Acknowledge people when they complete a section of the workshop content. Even acknowledge the audience for choosing to attend your seminar.

 By increasing positive emotions through sincere acknowledgment, I create joy, anticipation, and affirmation.

Making It Mine

Here is an exercise in "heart technology." This technique reframes negative thoughts into the powerful emotional states of appreciation and acknowledgment. You can practice it during rush hour, when standing in a long line, or in any other potentially stressful situation.

One by one, acknowledge the blessings in your life. Visualize and verbalize your appreciation for family, friends, kids, grandkids, siblings, your job, the car you drive, the house you live in, and so on. Appreciate all the big and small things in your life. Then, think of specific people you would like to acknowledge. Mentally express your gratitude for their contribution to your life.

Do this "heart" exercise daily until it becomes part of your thinking. Soon it will transfer to your training and teaching situations. You will soon sense the value of using appreciation and acknowledgment during your presentations.

Reach for the Stars!

Use the stars below to monitor your progress.

I have this tip
down cold!

It is familiar
territory.

This tip feels like a
new pair of shoes.

In the box, draw an icon or write key words that represent Acknowledge Participants.

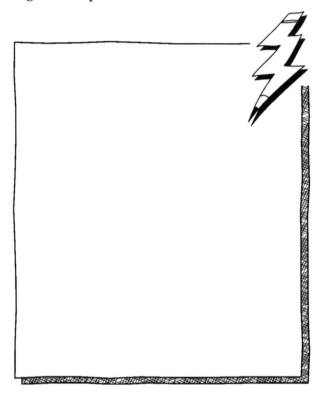

Thinking It Over

Rewrite the metacognitive statement from page 68. Enlarge or bold key words or phrases.

_____

_____

_____

_____

_____

Record any enhancements you have made to Acknowledge Participants, as well as your plans for implementing this HotTip.

Enhancements:_____

_____

_____

_____

_____

Implementation plans:_____

_____

_____

_____

_____

> I attribute
> most of
> my success
> to simply
> showing up.
>
> —Woody Allen

Take Care
of Number 1

Do not neglect your own physical and emotional preparation and maintenance.

Just as important as the content and logistics of your presentation is the care you take of yourself before and during the time you speak. Here are a few suggestions:

Make sure you are well hydrated: Drink plenty of water the day before your event. During the event, keep a bottle or pitcher of water near you.

Enjoy music: Prior to the presentation, turn on your favorite tunes and let the music set your frame of mind.

Power up: During breaks, nibble on a high-protein bar or other nutritional snack to sustain your physical energy.

Stay grounded: Place photographs of family, friends, and favorite places in a conspicuous spot. View them often, and allow the memories to comfort, inspire, and ground you.

Breathe: A series of deep breaths lowers your heart rate and supplies your body with ample oxygen.

 I choose to be my very best
in order to give my very best.

Making It Mine

Complete this short exercise to determine how well you take care of yourself before and during your presentations. Check the appropriate response.

1. **I drink plenty of water before and during my presentation. Water is always available.**
   ❏ Always ❏ Sometimes ❏ Rarely

2. **I purposely play music to prepare myself mentally.**
   ❏ Always ❏ Sometimes ❏ Rarely

3. **I eat nutritional snacks to maintain a high level of energy.**
   ❏ Always ❏ Sometimes ❏ Rarely

4. **I use photos of my family or others for inspiration and comfort.**
   ❏ Always ❏ Sometimes ❏ Rarely

5. **I breathe deeply and slowly to relax and prepare.**
   ❏ Always ❏ Sometimes ❏ Rarely

Now ask yourself this, "What do I need to do in order to take care of myself before and during my next presentation?"

Reach for the Stars!

Use the stars below to monitor your progress.

I have this tip down cold!

It is familiar territory.

This tip feels like a new pair of shoes.

In the box, draw an icon or write key words that represent Take Care of Number 1.

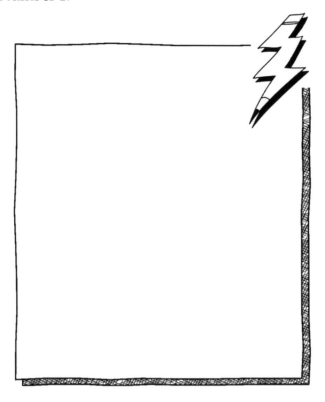

Thinking It Over

Rewrite the metacognitive statement from page 72. Enlarge or bold key words or phrases.

_____

_____

_____

_____

_____

Record any enhancements you have made to Take Care of Number 1, as well as your plans for implementing this HotTip.

Enhancements:_____

_____

_____

_____

_____

Implementation plans:_____

_____

_____

_____

_____

> It's your attitude and not your aptitude that determines your altitude.
>
> —Zig Ziglar

Enhance Learning through Music

Use music to add interest and increase learning.

Music powerfully affects learners. Some studies suggest that baroque music may enhance comprehension and retention of content (Rose and Nicholl 1998; Campbell 1997). Try playing baroque music softly as you present and while participants review or reflect on the content. Although the learning effect may not be universal, we have found baroque music helps participants to relax and focus.

Other styles produce other results. For example, upbeat popular music played during breaks and transitions energizes your participants. You can also use music to soothe, inspire, create a mood, signal transitions, and evoke emotion. Sound effects and theme songs create a sense of novelty and fun. Experiment to discover the effects of music and how you can use it to your best advantage.

By artfully applying music, I increase audience learning and enhance my delivery.

Making It Mine

If you have yet to gather a collection of music for your next presentation, start now. Make a list of music you think might be appropriate. Consider what music to play as participants arrive, when they are in transit from activity to activity, during breaks, and as they leave. Also, think about sound effects to enhance key points. Here are some ideas:

Opening: To set the right mood, carefully select 20 minutes of music to play prior to the start of your presentation. Jazz, swing, and light rock are a few of our favorites.

Fun: Play the theme song from the TV series *Bonanza* as your audience "gallops" through the handout to see what is in it.

Logistics: Use an upbeat song as a signal to regroup the audience after a break. Inform people that when they hear a particular song, the break is over.

Reach for the Stars!

Use the stars below to monitor your progress.

I have this tip down cold!

It is familiar territory.

This tip feels like a new pair of shoes.

In the box, draw an icon or write key words that represent Enhance Learning through Music.

Thinking It Over

Rewrite the metacognitive statement from page 76. Enlarge or bold key words or phrases.

_____
_____
_____
_____
_____

Record any enhancements you have made to Enhance Learning through Music, as well as your plans for implementing this HotTip.

Enhancements:_____

_____

_____

_____

_____

Implementation plans:_____

_____

_____

_____

_____

Let him step to the music that he hears.

—Henry D. Thoreau

Use Props

Use visible and invisible objects as learning aids.

If a picture is worth a thousand words, then a prop is worth a thousand mental associations. Props give a three-dimensional feel to your presentation. Using props to represent concepts solidifies participants' learning. Visible, tangible objects such as a picture frame, string, a molecular structure, an arrow, a hat, a puppet or stuffed animal, puzzle pieces, or oversized glasses add a concrete, metaphoric dimension to abstract concepts.

Even invisible props in the form of hand motions are useful. Have participants pretend to fashion spheres in midair, use a keyboard at their table, hold a phone to their ear, or pick up a utensil. Such actions will give them a feel for the information.

Choose props purposefully. Your kinesthetic learners appreciate something to hold and manipulate as you speak, so place Koosh elastic rubber balls on the tables. Put juggling scarves on the tables. Using the scarves at break time promotes collaborative fun and challenges your participants to do something they may never have done before.

 I connect concepts with concrete objects so my participants can see and feel their learning.

Making It Mine

Make a list of objects you could use to aid participants' learning. Think of everyday items you have around your house or garage. You may even want to stroll through a toy store for additional ideas.

_____   _____
_____   _____
_____   _____
_____   _____
_____   _____
_____   _____
_____   _____
_____   _____
_____   _____
_____   _____

Reach for the Stars!

Use the stars below to monitor your progress.

I have this tip down cold!

It is familiar territory.

This tip feels like a new pair of shoes.

In the box, draw an icon or write key words that represent Use Props.

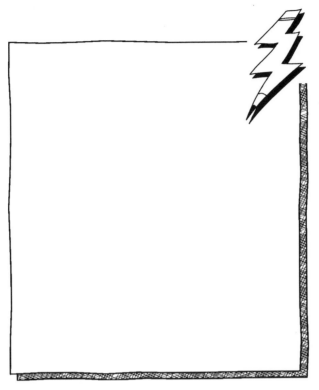

Thinking It Over

Rewrite the metacognitive statement from page 80. Enlarge or bold key words or phrases.

_____

_____

_____

_____

_____

Record any enhancements you have made to Use Props, as well as your plans for implementing this HotTip.

Enhancements:_____

_____

_____

_____

_____

Implementation plans:_____

_____

_____

_____

_____

> So simplify the information as much as possible, and use audiovisual aids to speed up the [learning] process!
>
> —Dr. Albert Mehrabian

Set the Stage

Create an ambiance conducive to learning.

Your presentation begins the moment your audience walks into the room. What they see, hear, and feel influences their receptivity and readiness to learn. Create a positive ambiance with these suggestions:

➤ Play jazz or other upbeat, popular, age-appropriate music for 20 to 30 minutes before you begin.

➤ Place toys, colorful markers, Koosh elastic rubber balls, puzzle pieces, small wooden blocks, eyeglasses, or other topic-related objects on the tables.

➤ Post inspirational sayings, truth signs, and content-related icons on the walls.

➤ Place a welcome sign (or other greeting) on the front door, on the floor at the entrance, or at the front of the room. (Also personally greet participants.)

➤ Display props and other visual aids on a table at the front of the room to heighten curiosity.

 I create a warm, inviting, and intriguing atmosphere for learning.

Making It Mine

Set the Stage for your friend, spouse, or significant other. Orchestrate a memorable evening by creating a particular atmosphere. Create the desired mood with music, lighting, food, location, candles, etc.

What other things could you do to set the stage for this evening?

_____

_____

_____

_____

_____

_____

_____

_____

_____

Reach for the Stars!

Use the stars below to monitor your progress.

I have this tip
down cold!

It is familiar
territory.

This tip feels like a
new pair of shoes.

In the box, draw an icon or write key words that represent Set the Stage.

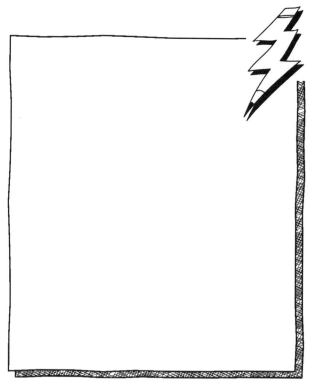

Thinking It Over

If your room were a stage set for learning, what would it look, sound, and feel like? Record your ideas.

Looks like: _____

_____

Sounds like: _____

_____

Feels like: _____

_____

Record any enhancements you have made to Set the Stage, as well as your plans for implementing this HotTip.

Enhancements:_____

_____

_____

_____

_____

Implementation plans:_____

_____

_____

_____

_____

All the world's a stage!

—William Shakespeare

Surf the
Unexpected Wave

Facilitate, rather than immediately redirecting, unexpected comments or interactions.

*S*urfing refers to your flexibility in switching topics to meet participants' immediate needs for information. As an effective presenter, you carefully plan your content and process to meet the diverse needs of your audience. Inevitably, however, moments arise when participants—through interactions, questions, or comments—travel to new or parallel areas of thought. This is your opportunity to go with them, to surf, to catch their thought wave, and to facilitate it.

Surfing is one solution to meeting the specific needs of your participants. Ask questions such as, "What other thoughts do you have about that?" to uncover information they already know. Allow yourself to surf through the unknown agenda with your audience. You may be pleasantly surprised at where it leads! Stay out in the water with them for a short while, then gently guide them back to the beach. Remember, surf just long enough to meet the immediate need, then return to your content.

By surfing, I allow myself the flexibility to connect with the immediate needs of my participants.

Making It Mine

Search out your most abstract-random friend—the most feeling-oriented, go-with-the-flow, global thinker you know. Take him or her to lunch or dinner, or just chat over a cup of coffee. As you enjoy your friend's company, carefully observe his or her random thinking. Notice how your friend switches topics in an instant. See the waves of random thinking and ride with them. Surf with the randomness and pursue the various paths of thought. Ask purposeful questions to promote your friend's thinking about each new topic. Then, after a short time, lead the way back to the beach, back to the original topic—that is, if you can remember it after doing all that surfing!

Reach for the Stars!

Use the stars below to monitor your progress.

I have this tip down cold!

It is familiar territory.

This tip feels like a new pair of shoes.

In the box, draw an icon or write key words that represent Surf the Unexpected Wave.

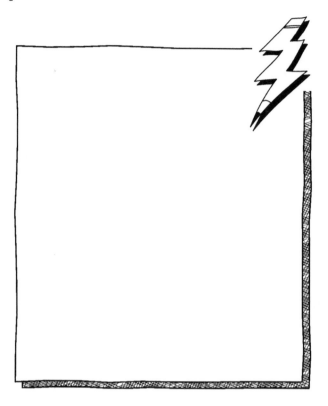

Thinking It Over

To prepare for your next "surfing" episode, consider moments during your presentation when related or tangential topics might arise. What are they? List them and determine how you will surf from there back to your planned content.

1. _____

_____

Surf: _____

_____

2. _____

Surf: _____

3. _____

Surf: _____

Record any enhancements you have made to Surf the Unexpected Wave, as well as your plans for implementing this HotTip.

Enhancements: _____

_____

_____

Implementation plans: _____

_____

_____

> The greatest thing
> in this world
> is not so much
> where we are, but
> in what direction
> we are moving.
>
> —Oliver W. Holmes

Conquer the Fear

Use strategies to overcome the natural fear of public speaking.

Some would argue that the number-one fear in the United States is speaking in public. This fear is common to both rookie and veteran presenters. In our experience, we have found we can eliminate most of the nervousness through simple preparation and active rehearsal, a little more through deep breathing, and whatever remains through mental preparation. Mark Twain, one of the highest-paid speakers of his time, said, "It takes me at least three weeks to prepare an impromptu speech."

Here are the strategies:

- ➤ Spend the time and energy to prepare and rehearse, especially your opening, since this is the time when the fear is greatest.

- ➤ Take deep breaths and hold each for four or five seconds. Exhale with a controlled, slow release. Then inhale deeply and repeat.

- ➤ Silence the negative voice in your head. Feed your mind positive affirmations, ones that give you power and confidence. (For example, *I am glad to be here. Today will be a valuable day for everyone. I anticipate a day of fun, learning, and adventure.*)

- ➤ Finally, focus your mind on your audience. This way you will not have time to worry about yourself.

I have the necessary tools and strategies to conquer my fears. By preparing, rehearsing, breathing, and managing my thoughts, I take control of my fears in any situation.

Making It Mine

The biggest battle with fear occurs in the first few moments of a presentation. Mentally rehearse those moments, seeing and feeling yourself being calm and collected. What are you saying to yourself? Capture this positive internal dialogue for later rehearsal.

_____

_____

_____

_____

Reach for the Stars!

Use the stars below to monitor your progress.

I have this tip down cold!

It is familiar territory.

This tip feels like a new pair of shoes.

In the box, draw an icon or write key words that represent Conquer
the Fear.

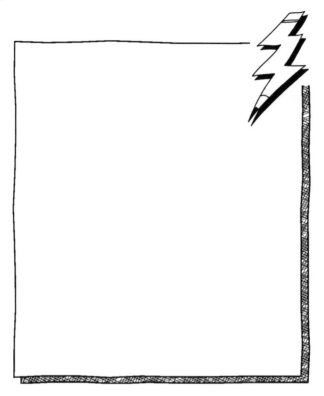

Thinking It Over

Rewrite the metacognitive statement from
the previous page. Enlarge or bold key words
or phrases.

_____

_____

_____

_____

_____

Record any enhancements you have made to Conquer the Fear, as well as your plans for implementing this HotTip.

Enhancements: _____

_____

_____

_____

_____

Implementation plans: _____

_____

_____

_____

_____

FEAR:

False

Expectations

Appearing

Real

—Michael Wall

Keep Pruning

Continually refine your content and process.

Have you ever thought that your last presentation, talk, or speech was perfect? Well, as you know, no presentation can be. "You are either green and growing, or ripe and rotten," as the saying goes. You change; audiences change; attitudes change. Pruning your presentation keeps it current and fresh both for the minds of your listeners and for you as the presenter.

A good rule of thumb is to modify about 5 percent of your presentation each time you present it. You could make minor changes in the content, such as updating information, finding a better story or comic strip, or using a clearer metaphor. Or you might modify your process. For example, you might ask a more direct question. You might even change a skill element. You could stand differently, speak with different intonation, or use slides instead of overheads.

Modifications keep your presentation alive, current, and constantly improving. So go ahead and prune your next presentation, nourish it, fine-tune it. You and your audience will be glad you did.

> I continually prune my presentation. I search for new ways to help my participants grasp the content more easily and on a deeper level. Just like me, my presentation is alive and growing.

Making It Mine

Grab a folder and label it "Fresh Air." For one month, scan a variety of magazines, newspapers, journals, and advertisements. Collect interesting or startling facts, quotations, cartoons, statements, and stories you think could be integrated into your presentations. Gather as many as you can throughout the month. Here is a rule of thumb: 20 to 30 artifacts yield about five to seven that can be incorporated into any presentation you do.

Continue saving tidbits for a year, adding whatever catches your eye. Having heightened your awareness, you will notice even more fresh air in things people say to you. Before you know it, you will have a folder full of golden, fresh air to grab the attention and interest of your participants for years to come. This is one folder you will cherish and use often.

Reach for the Stars!

Use the stars below to monitor your progress.

I have this tip down cold!

It is familiar territory.

This tip feels like a new pair of shoes.

In the box, draw an icon or write key words that represent Keep Pruning.

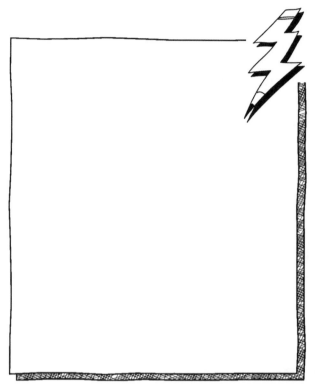

Thinking It Over

What 5 percent will you change for your next presentation? Will you modify the content, the process, or your delivery? Consider your options, write them down, and begin a process of continual improvement now.

_____

_____

_____

_____

_____

HotTips for Speakers ©2002 Zephyr Press, Tucson, AZ • 800-232-2187 • www.zephyrpress.com

Record any enhancements you have made to Keep Pruning, as well as your plans for implementing this HotTip.

Enhancements:_____

_____

_____

_____

_____

Implementation plans:_____

_____

_____

_____

_____

Kaizen:
Japanese word for small, seemingly insignificant, ongoing, continuous, and never-ending improvements.

—Mark Reardon

Balance Gum and Chewing

Use "gum" and "chewing" as metaphors for determining the blend of content and process.

As a presenter or facilitator, you orchestrate two contextual levels during any seminar, workshop, or training session. You design the brain-to-brain, or content, level (the gum); and you design the heart-to-heart, or process, level (the chewing).

How much time should you allocate to each level in a given presentation? The answer lies in your overall cognitive and affective objectives. For example: Imagine you are delivering information at the awareness and knowledge stages of learning, the two earliest stages of learning a new skill (Garmston 1997). You would devote about 70 percent of the time to the gum (content), and the remaining 30 percent for chewing (process). If your goal is to enhance application, then give the audience gum for the first 50 percent of the time, and let them chew for the other 50 percent. If changing values and beliefs is your objective, then devote the first 50 percent to chewing, and use the second half for gum. In other words, you might begin with a simulation activity (chewing) and then debrief (gum) to discover the learning.

Think about your content and process using this metaphor. You will quickly discover the most effective balance for each type of presentation you do.

My audience is diverse and unique. I can maximize their learning by consciously balancing content and process.

Making It Mine

Take a piece of your favorite gum. Open the wrapper and place the gum in the palm of your hand. Does it give you any enjoyment by just sitting there? No. It may look good, but the real reward of gum (content) comes in the chewing (process). Now put the piece of gum into your mouth and let it sit there. What do you notice? Flavor? Texture? Shape? Size? This represents adding new elements of the content (gum). The rewards of the process have just begun. Now chew your gum. What new things do you notice? Bursts of flavor? Juiciness? New textures? A far richer and more rewarding experience is yours because you are chewing. The value of gum comes in chewing. The same is true of your information. Next time, offer your audience three pieces of gum (three main ideas) and let them chew, chew, chew.

Reach for the Stars!

Use the stars below to monitor your progress.

I have this tip down cold!

It is familiar territory.

This tip feels like a new pair of shoes.

In the box, draw an icon or write key words that represent Balance Gum and Chewing.

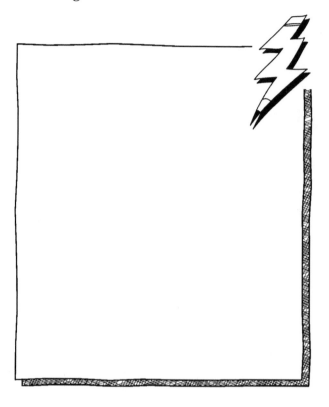

Thinking It Over

Rewrite the metacognitive statement from the previous page. Enlarge or bold key words or phrases.

_____

_____

_____

_____

_____

Record any enhancements you have made to Balance Gum and Chewing, as well as your plans for implementing this HotTip.

Enhancements:_____

_____

_____

_____

_____

Implementation plans:_____

_____

_____

_____

_____

> " Audience interest,
> questions, and
> comments are
> my best editors.
>
> —Arden Bercovitz "

Make Cheat Sheets

Use carefully placed notes to assist you in remembering what to say or do.

Cheat sheets build confidence and assist you in remembering what to say or do. Here are three simple techniques. (They may be the only three you will ever need!)

Flip charts: Write very lightly with pencil on the paper. The audience will not be able to see the words. During the presentation, you can simply retrace the penciled words with colored markers.

Overheads: Jot notes on the overhead cell protector sheet. Flip Frames protector sheets for overhead transparencies (sold by 3M) have a two-inch opaque border on which you can write plenty of notes.

Front table: Hang chart paper containing your key information on the front of the first row of tables. You can read the sheets, but the audience cannot see them.

Cheat sheets are also great learning tools. In a short time you will have memorized the information on your cheat sheets through visual display and repetition. Go ahead and cheat a little! Consider it a learning technique!

> I deliver information with confidence because I know it is right in front of me.

Making It Mine

Think of your body as a cheat sheet. Imagine that you need to purchase seven items from the grocery store: watermelon, mustard, onions, ice cream, toilet paper, milk, and gum. Connect each item to a specific part of your body using vivid, colorful images:

> ➤ Put the watermelon on your head and visualize the mustard dripping out of your ears.

> ➤ Place a big onion in each eye, which makes you cry.

> ➤ Stuff scoops of ice cream into your mouth.

> ➤ Have the toilet paper rolling out of your hands.

> ➤ Finally, stand in a puddle of milk with gum stuck to the bottom of your feet.

When you walk into the store, think of the body parts, and the items will surface visually in your mind. Try this with your own shopping list. You can use the same strategy to hang important facts in your presentation on parts of your body.

Reach for the Stars!

Use the stars below to monitor your progress.

I have this tip down cold!

It is familiar territory.

This tip feels like a new pair of shoes.

In the box, draw an icon or write key words that represent Make Cheat Sheets.

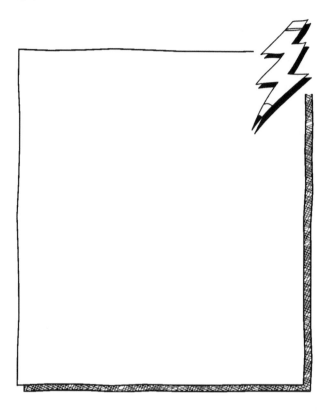

Thinking It Over

What key points in your next presentation do you want to remember? Jot them down. Now use your body as a cheat sheet, attaching your ideas vividly to parts of your body.

Point 1: _____

_____

Visualization: _____

_____

Point 2: _____

_____

Visualization: _____

_____

Point 3: _____

_____

Visualization: _____

_____

Record any enhancements you have made to Make Cheat Sheets, as well as your plans for implementing this HotTip.

Enhancements: _____

_____

Implementation plans: _____

_____

> The human brain is a wonderful organ. It starts to work as soon as you are born, and doesn't stop until you get up to deliver a speech.
>
> —George Jessel

Further Learning

Campbell, D. 1997. *The Mozart Effect.* New York: Avon Books.

Consalvo, C. 1992. *Workplay.* King of Prussia, Pa.: Organizational Design and Development.

Covey, S. 1991. *Principle-Centered Leadership.* New York: Simon and Schuster.

Decker, B. 1991. *You've Got to Be Believed to Be Heard.* New York: St. Martin's Press.

DePorter, B. 1992. *Quantum Learning.* New York: Dell.

DePorter, B., S. Singer-Nourie, and M. Reardon. 1999. *Quantum Teaching: Orchestrating Student Success.* Needham Heights, Mass.: Allyn & Bacon.

Garmston, R. 1997. *The Presenter's Fieldbook: A Practical Guide.* Norwood, Mass.: Christopher-Gordon Publishers.

Goleman, D. 1997. *Emotional Intelligence.* New York: Bantam Books.

Harmin, Merrill. 1995. *Inspiring Active Learning.* Edwardsville, Ill.: Inspiring Strategies Institute.

Jensen, E. 1994. *The Learning Brain.* Del Mar, Calif.: Turning Point.

————. 1995. *Brain-Based Learning and Teaching.* Del Mar, Calif.: Turning Point.

Lambert, L. 1995. *The Constructivist Leader.* New York: Teachers College Press.

Nadel, L., J. Wilmer, and E. M. Kurtz. 1984. Cognitive Maps and Environmental Context. In *Context and Learning,* edited by P. Balsam and A. Tomie. Mahwah, N.J.: Lawrence Erlbaum Associates.

Ostrander, S., and L. Schroeder. 2000. *Super-Learning.* New York: Delacorte Press.

Rose, C., and M. J. Nicholl. 1998. *Accelerated Learning for the Twenty-First Century.* New York: Delacorte Press.

Rosenfield, M., and B. Gilmartin. 1991. Effect of Target Proximity on the Open Loop Accommodative Response. *Optometry and Vision Science* 67(2): 74–79.